Through Apocalypse To Grace

OrangeBooks Publication

Smriti Nagar, Bhilai, Chhattisgarh - 490020

Website: **www.orangebooks.in**

Through Apocalypse To Grace

POOJA FRANCIS

OrangeBooks Publication

www.orangebooks.in

You're trembling, as if the storm is near...
everything is fading.
Trying to catch your breath, your head's spinning.
Your heart, it's beating too fast,
and you're gasping for life.
You feel like giving up.
You feel like there's no way out.
You feel the darkness taking its place.
You try to yell, but nothing comes out.
Only silence....

I know that we have our own kind of apocalypse and we
keep saying the end is near, isn't it?
Yet!

You get back on your feet, undaunted.

You feel the fire rising within you, and you rise.

You feel the power, the hope.

The flames in you burst brilliantly, devouring every darkness... and you rise fearlessly just like a phoenix,

......you RISE WITH GRACE.

Acknowledgment

To my grandparents, Michael Francis and Stella Francis, thank you for the memories.

My parents who've always been there to support me. Thank you for your love and guidance.

To all my uncles and aunts, (bua and phupha) thank you for always helping me and appreciating me.

I want to thank all my cousins, my brother Pratik Michael Francis, and my sissy Pragya Venessa Francis, for always making me smile.

I want to sincerely thank Yoana Augustine, for guiding and reading early drafts. Thank you for being there for me. She stood by me during every struggle and all my successes. 'Thank you for your awesomeness.' Editors, you may cut this line.

My friends, who are just like my Family, whether we live close, states apart or in two different continents, you all were always there for me and never judged me. THANK YOU, Stevie Flood, Asmita Seth, Darlene Gregg, Ritchel Montana, Anna Marie Estrada, Lori Carter, Madhurima Roychawdhury, Paulami Debnath, Sharon Alfred, Robbie J Sherrah, Hanlie Robbertse , JP Louise, Jay Long, Amir Shahab Chishti, Janine Tamis, MJ Kociss, Reggie Nulan, Manul Kamthan, Rihan Mustafa, Arveena Soni, Danny

Jason, Coleen C Kimbro,Jai Evergreen, Dave Konkin, Luna Rose, Luna Deity, Dalena Duco,Grant Wass, Ally Ricaud, Kathy Cook Starta, James Sterling, Mobin Sam Thomas, Paula Luise, Sammie Payne, Sarah Kacala, Margie Watts, Shannon Arthium, Laura Hughes, Shawna Heaton and Samantha Jo.

Thank you so much for your never ending love and support. I have never met some of you, but your care and kindness cannot be expressed in mere words. Thank you for Inspiring me. Online friends are real friends too.

You all mean the world to me. I love you.

Special thanks to those who follow my pages, you are the reason that I am here; your kindness and support means everything to me.

Dedicated to Prashant Francis.
(19th Sep, 1974- 2nd October, 2020)
To my uncle (chacha) I miss you.

I close my eyes, hoping and praying for you to come back. I open my eyes, realising that you are never coming back.

I close my eyes, remembering and cherishing all the memories.
I open my eyes, and I see how this life made you suffer.

I close my eyes, I see how you never left my hand in any situation.

I open my eyes, I see you in deep peaceful sleep, holding your hand, and having no choice but simply to let go.

Contents

1. Don't Let The Darkness Fool You......................1

2. Speak Up!......................3

3. Warrior 4

4. Don't Give Up......................5

5. Tired......................7

6. You're Enough......................9

7. Love Needs Love. 10

8. Free Yourself......................11

9. Not Every Silence Is Peaceful. 12

10. Life Goes On. 13

11. Wrong Battles......................14

12. Monster 15

13. Listen To Your Heart 16

14. Wildflower......................17

15. You......................18

16. Gently......................19

17. Moon......................20

18. Self Love......................21

19. Poetry......................22

20. Numb......................23

21. You're Not A Failure. 24

22. Soul 25

23. Empath 26

24. I Fell 27

25. Exhausted. 28

26. Grief 29

27. Sensitivity Is Strength. 30

28. Love 31

29. It Hurts 32

30. Phoenix. 34

31. Shine. 35

32. Betrayal. 36

33. Wounded Love. 37

34. US. 38

35. Rise. 39

36. Forgive Yourself. 40

37. Buried Love 41

38. Your Emotions Are Valid. 42

39. Moon And Stars. 43

40. Burning love. 44

41. I Should've Loved Myself. 45

42. Run. 46

43. Freedom. 48

44. Home In Hell. 49

45. Weak In The Knees. 50

46. I tried.. 51

47. Heavier.. 52

48. No Darkness Can Touch You. 53

49. Walk Away 54

50. Void... 55

51. Walls 56

52. You Shine 57

53. Storm... 58

54. Inner Child... 59

55. Scars.. 60

56. Broken... 61

57. Selenophile.. 62

58. Coffin Nails 63

59. Safe Place.. 64

60. Memories... 66

61. Right Person, Wrong Time.............................. 67

62. Fallen Stars.. 68

63. Men. 69

64. You Care. 70

65. Found Myself. 71

66. Cold... 72

67. Worth It. 73

68. It's Just You. 74

69. Innocence. 75

70. Silence... 76

71. Who's There For You? 77

72. Fragments 78

73. Demon 79

74. Feel 80

75. I'm Done 81

76. Scared 82

77. They Change 83

78. Heaven And Hell 84

79. Meaningless Words 85

80. Strength 86

81. Too Much 87

82. Cage 88

83. It Takes Time 89

84. Thoughts 90

85. Stranger 91

86. Please, Don't Do It 92

87. It Wasn't Our Fault 93

88. You Deserve Love 95

89. Apocalypse 96

90. Healing 97

91. Safe 98

92. Don't Let Them In 99

93. It Is, What It Is 100

94. Silence 101

95. Within Me 102

96. Can You?.. 103

97. Healing Is Real 104

98. You Feel It.. 105

99. Blame Games 106

100. Saved 107

101. Wings... 108

102. Treachery 110

103. Survived... 111

Don't Let The Darkness Fool You

No matter how hard it gets
No matter how overwhelming,
No matter how depressing,
No matter how negative.
Don't let the darkness fool you, because it does!!
It makes you blind, it feeds you lies!!
It knows hope would never leave so it tries to cover up.
It knows that no matter how small or how dim.
Hope stays!!
Hear me out,
Keep that fire of hope burning
However small.
However hidden.

Speak Up!

Trauma is possessive.
It steals your voice, your thoughts, your vision, your life.

You become a prisoner.

One thing that it cannot steal is your faith,
hope and courage.

Speak up!!

The words that have left you frozen for years,
might be the only words that will set you free.

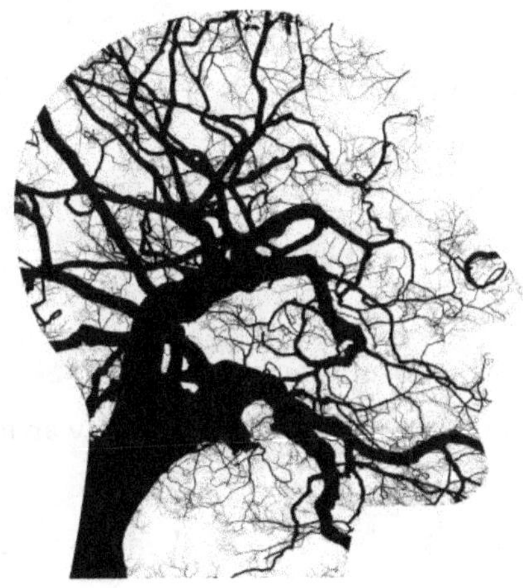

Pooja Francis

Warrior

If you get up every morning without
anybody knowing, how much effort it took,

Just to get out of that damn bed, You're a warrior.

If you're holding on, even if every bone inside you is
collapsing, You're a warrior.

While giving up is the easiest thing to do,
You're still dragging yourself to reach your goal,

Darling, you're a warrior.

You bleed, you crumble, you fall, you fail,
you shatter, And then you rise,

You're a warrior.

Those weapons, knives,
guns Doesn't make you a strong warrior

Sometimes, when you lay them down and
walk away, You become a warrior.

Don't Give Up

Sometimes the road gets too rough

You have no choice, but to get through that rough patch.
In times like these, I hope you don't give up.

No matter how positive you are,

Some things … will go wrong and out of your hands, In
times like these, I hope you don't give up.

Sometimes the person who was your last hope,

walks away. Never mind,

Because sometimes when people grow,

they grow apart and they fade,

In times like these, I hope you don't give up.

The trees you look around were just a tiny seed one day,
And you say you don't believe in miracles?

You're just growing.

So please, I hope you don't give up

Sometimes when you take one step forward,

Life pulls you five steps backwards

Don't worry,

Even though life hasn't been fair, but when it pulls you
back, It is only because you're going to reach in some
better place,

So please don't ever give up.

Tired

I feel everything deeply,
Though my heart is tired, but my soul?
Keep fighting.
And when I look at myself, I feel tired.

Sensitive souls don't have it easy in this world.
Walls so high, but no one cares enough to see all the
love behind it. All alone, when I look at myself, I feel
tired.

It's weighing me down, drowning me deep in the dark. I
keep calling, and no one answers.
Somehow, I muster all the strength,
and I tell myself, It's not over yet.
I'll get through it.
No matter what,I'll rise

Yes I still feel tired …
So I will rest

No! I won't quit.

You're Enough

I understand that the cleft between who you are, and who you want to be can be very muddled.

It can make you feel drowning in the dark and doubt. But I tell you, cherish it.

Adorn the gap with hope and faith. Trust yourself even if no one does. You have you and that's enough!!

Love Needs Love

Why do we confess or fall in love, like it's a crime?

Why can't love be a commitment, and people stay in love? Love also needs love, in order to grow

Don't fall in love,
Grow in love.

Free Yourself

When I tell you that you should never forget who you are. I hope you know, that I'm not talking about your

Bank account, report cards, percentage, expensive furniture, weight, colour, quantity of your friends, or how big your house is, or the school you went to.

No! They don't define you.

I'm talking about the real you. Raw you.

The one you've entombed by the weight of other peoples' desires. So

free yourself from their hypnotism.

Open your eyes!
Look at yourself!

Accept and love yourself.
Exactly where you are!

Trust me, only then you will see
your life changing and worth living.
Because life is short,
you are not supposed to exist – but live!

Not Every Silence Is Peaceful

Not every silence is peaceful.

Sometimes people withdraw themselves and become
numb and silent,

Only because,

They have so much to say.

Life Goes On

You need to keep moving forward.

Even with tears in your eyes,
Even with all the anger inside,
Even when the darkness is surrounding,
Even if you think you can't, Well...
Especially, when you think you can't.

Life goes on
You need to, too.

Wrong Battles

I feel so exhausted.
Everything seems so unfair.

How long can I bear it?
This room of doubts and insecurities.
I want to bleed my words,
But, all I feel is nothing at all.

Fighting this battle for a while now.
Maybe I should rest?

Or maybe,
I'm fighting the wrong battles.

Monster

Growing up in an emotionally abusive
environment can leave long lasting scars.

Those scars are not really visible,
But if you look into the depth of my soul,
You will see …
How they bleed.

You trapped me in the room of
Darkness, fear and broken dreams.

You took advantage of my innocence How slowly and
lovingly, you turned me into a monster.

And, I've been fighting with that monster ever since.

Listen To Your Heart

Listening to your heart is not a sign of
weakness or being too emotional and irrational.
Listening to your heart is more about peace and
serenity.I

understand, the voices are too loud,

But your heart, It whispers.

Your heart knows everything, It will never lie.
It can heal every scar.
It's the mind, you need to silence it.

Listen to your heart...
For it's not just an organ…
It's your soul.

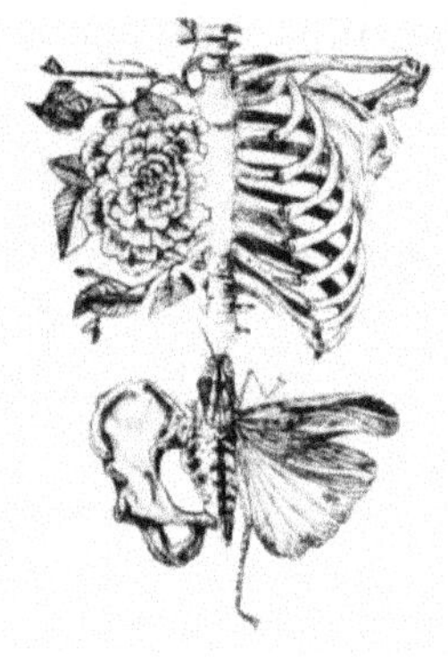

Wildflower

When you find yourself buried into the darkness I hope,
you muster up the strength to
grow and bloom like a wildflower.

You

You bring peace to my soul like a dove.

Your existence makes me believe in magic.

I love you with such a passion, that it's both a curse and
a blessing at the same time.

Gently

That little girl will always be attached to your soul,
searching for her lost innocence.

The stains of trauma never leave your soul. Be

gentle with her,

Healing takes time.

Sometimes in order to feel everything deeply and to let
go. You need to rip the band-aid very slowly and gently.

Moon

A moon is still a moon, even when it's in a different phase. And just like the moon,

I've loved you in all your phases.

Self Love

Building a home in someone else's heart will always
make you feel weak, and homesick.

Your own heart and soul is your home.
Decorate it with self love.

Poetry

I never knew Poetry, until I met you.
I never bled poetry, until you left me.

Numb

You inject your heart and soul with '
I don't care' You make it numb.
How long will you hide yourself?
How long will you pretend to be safe?

There will be a day when you will feel everything.
You will hear whispers which
will soon turn into loud noises.
Please understand,

You're making it worse.

You're Not A Failure

You think everything in your life has conspired against
your favour? You lock yourself in the chamber of self-
doubt and insecurities.

You're a sensitive soul,

Show some mercy to your soul.

Try again.

You're not failure,

As long as you keep trying.

Soul

My cold heart melts by the warmth of your soul.

Empath

To all those sensitive and empathetic souls.

I know life has been so unfair to you.

You feel so heavy.

Your heart is weighing you down.

Your soul is bruised with words that have hit you and
left a scar.

Even after all this, You show the world how deep your
love is.

How pure your compassion is.

You should be proud of yourself.

I Fell

I fell so hard for you, that even your coldness couldn't stop my heart from melting it.

Exhausted

Sometimes we get so exhausted being the person who
always stays when everyone leaves the room.

We get exhausted being the person who cares more. It

feels like we're so done being that backup friend.

So done, being the second choice when their plans didn't
work out.

We're tired of being the person who goes against our
nature just to see others happy.

For once we want to feel what it's like to be someone's
first choice. Isn't it?

Grief

If I let you kiss me,
You'll taste the grief I've been gulping down all my life.

Sensitivity Is Strength

Be a proud sensitive soul.
Don't bury your sensitivity,
don't hide it behind your walls.

Embrace it.

Your sensitivity is your strength.
Don't you dare think that it's your weakness.

How courageous you are, not afraid to dive into the
depths of your soul.

The world needs more people like you.

Love

I'm sorry if someone made you believe
that love is pain, It wasn't love.

Because love is always the cure.

It Hurts

Sometimes there's no insight.
There's no hope.

Your heart, it loves so hard. It was meant to ache.

You know deep down, this will pass.

So, you keep breathing, you keep trying.

You keep those shattered pieces of your heart inside the
cage.

Locked.

But, No matter what you do.
Sometimes

It.
just. hurts.

Phoenix

When life breaks you and hits you hard in the face.
Because, it will.

When life pushes you into the grave of your grief to let
you fall and die. When life leaves you all alone burning
and hurting with self-doubt. You

show it, how a phoenix is born with ashes.

You rise.

That's what you'll do,
EVERY. SINGLE. TIME.

Shine.

Some souls,
No matter how broken they are.

They smile.

No matter how long they've been stuck in darkness.

How beautifully they shine.

Betrayal

By keeping your heart inside a cage,
and calling it 'safe'.

You're hurting yourself.

By covering up your heart with a label saying 'I don't
care' You are ignoring and disrespecting your own
emotions.

And by turning your heart into a stone and against love
You're betraying your own soul.

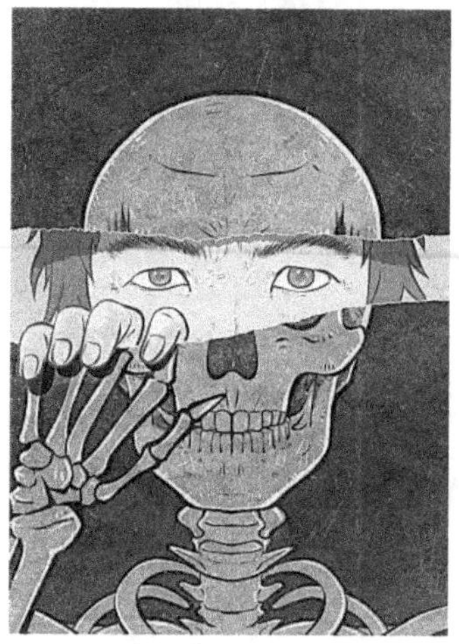

Wounded Love

Sometimes, no matter how wounded you are in love,
you don't want any cure.

You just hide those desires in a dark place,
and adore the beauty of those shattered pieces.

US

We're both damaged, and in this journey of healing,
I will love you endlessly.

I will guard and protect your heart just like mine.
For we are together in this.

We keep fighting our demons, We even lose at times.
But, we never give up.
One day, love will bring the demons down on its knees.
Because in this war.
Our love is the greatest weapon.

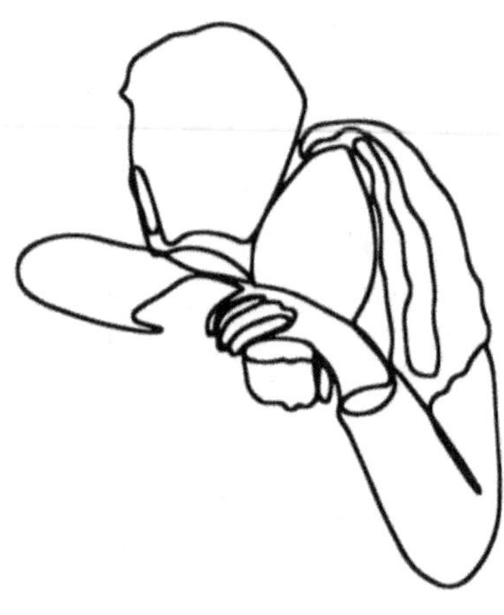

Rise

Promise yourself that,
No matter what you went through.

No matter how many times life pushes you back. No matter how many times you had to burn yourself down.
No matter how many times you made a mistake.

No matter how many times you didn't even feel like getting out of your bed.

No matter how many times you fell on your knees, just because you were strong for a long time.

And no matter how many times, you had to hide your scars and fake a smile.

YOU GET UP!
Even if it's for a millionth time.
You get up, because that's who you are. A warrior.
A phoenix.

You always get up and you rise.

Forgive Yourself

Sometimes, we make mistakes we thought we never
would.

Sometimes we sell a piece of ourselves,
we thought we'd never let go in the hands of a stranger.

It's okay,

Life is unpredictable.

It does not always give us what we want,

and sometimes to fill that emptiness.

We do things that might be completely against our
nature.

So now, regardless of what people say,

forgive yourself. You learn from it and you grow.

You don't deserve to be a prisoner of your mistakes.

Buried Love

As you dig a grave to bury this love of ours.
Please, bury my heart as well,
So that it stays attached to your love.

Forever in this darkness.

Pooja Francis

Your Emotions Are Valid

'You're thinking too much'

You must be tired hearing those words,
over and over again… '
Just get over it and move on'
Only if it was that easy.
So, you keep your emotions inside, Boiling.
You keep repressing it.
Those whispers, slowly becoming a Roar.

Hear me out, your emotions are valid!
They're worth listening to.
There's nothing wrong with you.
What happened to you, that's wrong.

Please understand this,
you matter! your feelings matter.

You don't know, someone out there might be dying to
hear your words.
You're already an inspiration.
Speak!!

Moon And Stars

Among the stars, you were always my moon.

I will always love you, even when you're far from full.

Burning love

You can hold your burning heart out for him.

A candle of hope burning and melting,
Leaving scars on your soul.

Waiting for him to see.

How you've loved him the way you've never been loved
before. Yet, It's not enough for him.

I Should've Loved Myself

I loved you unconditionally,
I loved you in every way I could, without any limits.

I loved you intensely.
I loved you, on your darkest days,
when you couldn't love yourself.

I loved you even when you were shouting with joy and
talking about the things you love,
with a spark in your eyes.
I loved you, when I missed you,
though you were right beside me. I

loved you, when you were slowly
slipping out from my arms.

I love you even when you were changing.

I've loved you in ways, I should've loved myself.

Run

You think there's no way out, and that you're locked up
inside your mind.
Burning.

Chained.
Blinded.
Darkness.

Fighting the demons inside.

Hear me out,
it's not you, who is inside that cage,
it's not you who is chained. It's them!!
They make you look as if it's you.
They take advantage of you.
But the reality is.

They're the ones locked and chained. They can't touch you. They scream to make you feel like you're deaf.

They keep making you feel like you're blind.

Do you hear me?

GET UP.

You were always free.

Leave that place.

Run.

Pooja Francis

Freedom

It was not the kind of freedom that I needed for myself.
But, the kind of freedom I needed from myself.

From my own thoughts.

From my chains.

From my past.

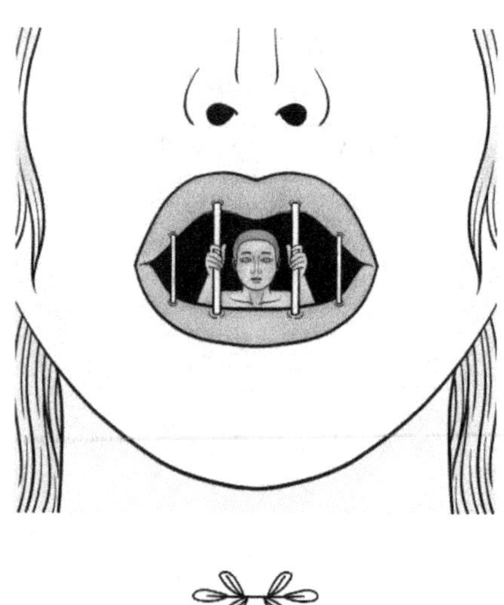

Home In Hell

You were supposed to love me unconditionally. You
were supposed to be my hiding place.

You talked, but you never listened.
Now your words are buried alive like a
bleeding scar in my soul.

The walls that made a home were the same walls that
created hell.
I've been finding a little peace in the fire I'm walking
through. All

you ever knew was loathe.

All I ever knew was love that …
That I'm still searching.

Weak In The Knees

No matter how strong, brave and courageous you are.
There is always that one person, Who makes you weak
in the knees.

Always.

I tried

I tried, but all I could say was nothing at all.

Silence.

Sometimes, the words we feel are not the same as the words we know.

Pooja Francis

Heavier

I wanted to be freed.
To fly and feel the wind.

I closed my eyes and I feel

The passion, the hope, wings, soaring high, never looking back. But reality hits me harder this time.

You never let me feel anything, you kept this heavy stone upon my heart, which was yours to carry.

I was only a child, trying to learn and grow.

Instead,

The stone kept growing bigger, and heavier every time.

No Darkness Can Touch You

As long as you believe in yourself, trust yourself and
love yourself, no matter what.

It might seem hard and impossible at times.
But, at the end of the day, all you have is yourself.

Hear me, as long as you accept yourself the way you are.

As long as you dive deep within your own soul and feel
your scar and decorate it gently with love.

No darkness can touch you!!

Walk Away

Walk away.
Lay down your weapons, and run.

You don't need to retaliate to every battle.
Sometimes winning a battle means,

Walking away.

Void

I've been trying to kill this empty space.

Searching for things to fill this void.

And, it's only killing me faster.

Walls

You came in and broke down my walls.
You understood each and every slab.
You opened my heart and called it home.

It was just an illusion, you see. It wasn't you.
It was me.

It was me, who let my guard down and gave you all of
me.

Now, I need to rebuild it, stronger this time.

You Shine

Sometimes, it gets dark for you to realize,
Just how beautifully you shine.

Storm

The thing with the storm is, That it won't pass,
Until and unless it changes you.

Inner Child

To my inner child,
I'm returning to you with love
and unconditional acceptance.

I hear your screams, I see your scars and I feel your fear.
I will heal you, my touch is safe.

I'm building a safe place, you will feel everything that
was stolen from you.

I promise you, you will heal.
You will feel loved.
In this storm, I will show peace.

Scars

Your scars tell a story.

About battles, Sufferings, tears, defeat, lost control,
sadness, hate, darkness,

But it also tells a lot about,

Peace, comfort, insights, joy, kindness, self-love,
and so much beauty.

Broken

Sometimes, the ones who were supposed to build us,
B r e a k us.

Selenophile

I'm here for you, as loyal as the moon.

I'm here for you, on days when you feel weak and on
days when your light is strong.

Moon showed me the meaning of love,
I'm here to prove it to you.

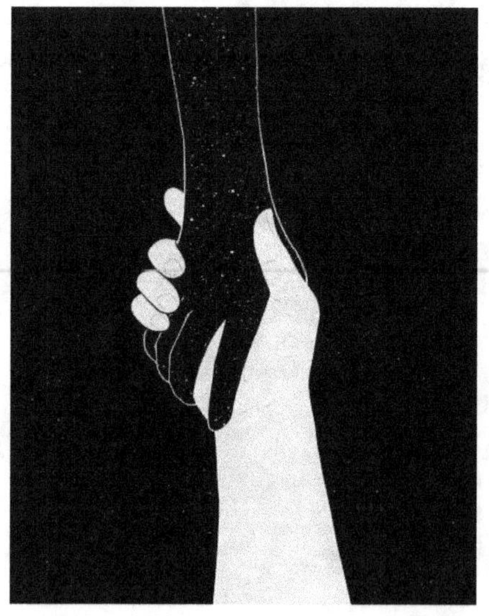

Coffin Nails

Trapped between my lips is a coffin nail.

Praying that one day,
the smoke will take away the memories with it.

Safe Place

You feel too much.

Too much in your bones.
An empath, they say.

Carrying every burden,
Walking amidst the storm.

Feeling the strong winds.
You've walked in so many shoes, Seen too many storms.
You deserve a safe place, let me embrace you. Let

go…

You don't need to carry this weight.
You deserve to be understood too.

You deserve love.

Memories

How can you let go of the memories,
if it is the memories holding you?

Right Person, Wrong Time

Someday, you'll meet a person,
who will start a fire within your soul.

Right person, at the wrong time, as they say.
There'll be nothing that you can do about it.
Sadly, they're the ones who will teach you how to let go.

Fallen Stars

Though, you are covered with scars.
Your ink flows like a fallen star.

Men

MEN!!

You're allowed to cry, you're allowed to release those
bottled-up emotions.

You're allowed to feel, You're allowed to ask for help.
You're a human being, we're all meant to feel.

No matter what they say, don't let them define you.

Your tears are not a sign of weakness,
it's a sign of bravery.

You Care

Sometimes, no matter how hard we yell that we don't care.

There's always this soft whisper, saying that we do.

Found Myself

Somewhere, while rescuing my soul from the darkness,
I found myself.

Cold

We're all born sensitive,
Don't you dare call it a sign of Weakness.
To feel and to be alive is a sign of strength.

Be gentle, embrace your sensitivity.

Don't let anything steal your grace, don't do that to
yourself. Remember, it's only death that causes one to
become cold.

Worth It

One of the hardest things you will have to do is to,

Peel off those layers of regret, pain, guilt, shame,
insecurities to find your soul.

It'll take time, it'll be painful, but It will be worth it.

Pooja Francis

It's Just You

They will say that they'll always be there for you.

Then there'll be a day, a fine Tuesday or Friday morning,
and it will be hard for you to get up,
Things might go bad again,
Anxiety and depression knocking at your door.

They will be busy, it might even be hard to open up.
At the end of the day, it will just be you.
That's why self-love is important.
That's why healing is important.
That's why self-acceptance is important.
That's why accepting your flaws and
embracing your soul is important.

Because, at the end of the day, it's just you.

Guess what, you're always enough.

Remember that!!

Innocence

You need to have patience for some people.

People who've been through a lot at an early age. Their innocence has witnessed a lot of fear.

Their innocence was taken away from them.

Have faith.

They're still trying.
They need a lot of assurance, before they let you in.

Their walls are too strong and too high.

Every day is a battle.

Have patience.

Silence

Such was the silence, so loud that no ink would have described it.

Who's There For You?

You're there for everyone, but who's there for you?

You always try to understand,

but who does that for you?

You give pieces of your own soul to heal them, and you
ache! Oh, how you ache,

but do they ever care how you heal?

You forgive, but then it's you, who is judged.

They leave, but you stay,

You make them a priority, but you're just an option.

You want to end it, you don't even want to breathe
anymore, yet you never let them fall short of breath.

Fragments

Don't forget the face of the person who showed you
hope, when you felt hopeless.

For some, it was no one but their own fragmented soul.

Demon

Loving you was like selling my soul to the demon.

Feel

Tears are sacred and real, let it fall.

Feel.

They show strength and honesty.
Fear the day when you let yourself become cold,
and freeze your tears.
That's how you will allow your soul to eat you alive.

I'm Done

Never again will I ever open up to someone,
or let them in.

It's like you let down your wall,
and they use those same bricks to hurt you.

Never will I ever open up,
for them to walk in and create a mess. I'm done.

Scared

You're scared too, aren't you?

Scared of the void that's surrounding your soul. You
keep fighting.

You build walls, and now there's no way out.

You tried, you showed them your feelings and they used
you. So you just shut everyone out.

It's scary, And it's sad, how much a human can hide
behind their smile.

They Change

It's sad how people decide that they don't
want you in their life anymore.
They change, and …

There's nothing you can do about it.

Heaven And Hell

It's heart-breaking, how you love them so much and they
stop caring about you.

You do so much for them, and they start taking you for
granted. You feel so much for them,

and they make you an option.

You're always there for them and they're not.

You love them so much, maybe they do too.

But only according to their needs.

There seems to be no way out, they make you live in
heaven and hell at the same time.

Meaningless Words

I had always found home in words.

Grew with them.

They were like a bandage upon my scars.

WORDS have the ability to heal, and also the power to
destroy. I'm still learning that words do lie.

Words are meaningless, if they're not backed by actions.

Words may heal, but when actions don't match

It gives a deep scar.

Strength

Sometimes, we know exactly what we deserve.

Our soul knows our potential, our needs, the fire burning within us. We just need the strength and support to act on it.

Too Much

It's strange,

When you build walls, they call you brave and strong.

Show a little vulnerability,
and you're just weak and too much.

Cage

It's not that people are scared to let their heart out of the cage…

Who doesn't love to be accepted and appreciated.

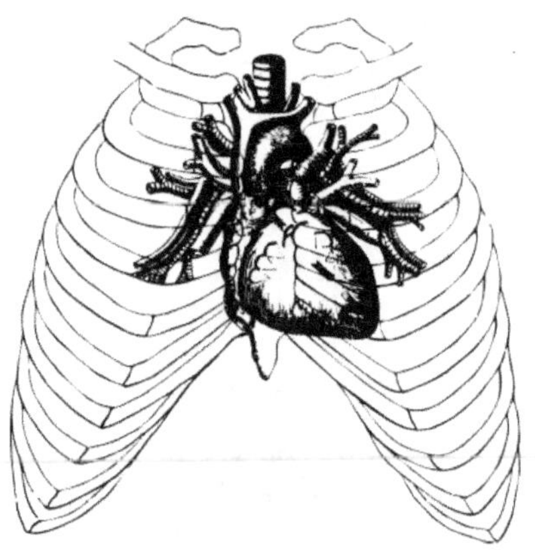

What people are scared of is how others use their vulnerability against them and destroy them.

It Takes Time

The reason why we feel so miserable is
that we're always in a hurry.

It takes time, remember that.

It took time to acknowledge and feel the pain, didn't it?

Just like that, it will take time to heal as well.

Thoughts

Don't let your repressed thoughts and emotions deceive you. There's a reason why they were repressed in the first place. Let them go, before they make you a prisoner.

Stranger

It's sad how you're portrayed as weak, and too much just
because you feel everything intensely.

It's scary, because sometimes when people don't accept
and love

you as you are, you start hating yourself.

What once felt like a blessing, becomes a curse.

When people don't understand you, your own soul feels
like a stranger.

Please, Don't Do It

If the only option you see is to die Let me tell you, it's a
lie.

If it's the pain, guilt, regret, anything,

Know that, I've sinned too.

If you can't get up,

Please let me help you.

Even if you are at your lowest,

Know that I've been there too.

Even if it's the darkest pit,

Know that, there's a light within you.

Please, don't do that to yourself,

Think about yourself.

Even if you feel weak and hopeless right now,

Know that, there's strength in your weakness.

Don't let the voices drown you.

Please don't do it.

It Wasn't Our Fault

My inner child, the way we were taught to live,

was wrong.

The way we had to drag our broken pieces,

just to survive a day, was wrong and unfair.

The words that were spoken to us, the way we were
neglected, the way we were thrown down,

the way we were treated.

It has nothing to do with us.

It's not our fault.

I need you to trust me,

Let me help and show you that you are loved, and you
are accepted. Don't be scared, we are home.

You Deserve Love

You deserve love that is gentle and certain.

Not brutal and unreliable.

You deserve love, that holds you and walks with you,
through the rough patch.

Not someone who abandons you in times of difficulties.

Apocalypse

We had our own universe, our own damn world.
To which you brought nothing, but destruction.

I had my own apocalypse.

Healing

Healing is messy.

It's crazy and it's dark.

You need to walk through your own storm.

Fall into the deepest and darkest corner of your painful ocean. It will be scary at first, but eventually you will learn how to swim.

Because you're brave.

But before taking the fall, you need to BELIEVE that you deserve to heal, and no matter what, you will RISE.

Safe

It was just a house, never a home.
Cold, heavy, distant, empty … yet loud,
But there was something about the walls …
The only thing that could keep me safe.

Don't Let Them In

We all have our demons, knocking at our souls.

Trying to get in, never giving up.

Don't listen, don't you dare feed them.

Once you let them in,

they will only choke and squeeze the life out of you,
leaving you with guilt, pain, anger and regret.

They won't stop until they eat every kindness, every
hope. You are stronger, don't let them in.

It Is, What It Is

It's terrible how they say, they won't do that to you…
But they don't even think once, when they do that to you.

Silence

It's sad how we get tired, just by caring so much,
only to get silence in return.

Within Me

I couldn't see people who were there for me, because all
I wanted was you to be there for me.

I couldn't see people who cared for me, because I wanted
you to care for me.

I couldn't feel any other embrace and affection, because I
wanted to feel you close.

I just wanted you, everything else was just an excuse or
escape.

I was so blinded, that I couldn't even see that everything
that I was searching for, has always been within me.

Can You?

So, you all talk about healing, and how being yourself is
enough, being all by yourself is enough.

Why don't you talk about how incredibly difficult it is?

What an enormous strength it requires to deal with your
own mind.

Especially, when your soul is sensitive and tired.

Believe it or not, we all need someone by our side.

Someone we can rely on.

Someone, we could run to when things get out of hand.
We're humans.

Solitude is important!

It is an essential part,

but you can't live like that forever, can you?

Healing Is Real

Mental illness is real.

What you feel is real and valid.

Anxiety is real, but don't stop believing in yourself.

Depression is real, but don't you dare give up on yourself. The storm that you're going through, is real.

Face it.

Your mistakes are your mistakes, it's real.

Learn, grow, let go.

Because, at the end…

Always remember and believe this,

Healing is also real.

You Feel It

What should I do with them?
Words!
They break you, they mend you.
It's such a mystery.
They say, 'I'm there for you'
Makes you feel safe, you hold onto it.
Then they leave, now what?
The same words that gave you hope,
are the same words now breaking your soul.
The next time, when someone says,
I'll be there for you.
You feel stuck, don't you?
You feel the emptiness in those words.

Blame Games

Sometimes people love you only because they can
control you.

They're there for you, because they can use you.

Be careful.

The moment you take your power back,

the moment you choose peace.

Their blame game starts.

Saved

Sometimes, warriors need to be saved too.

Wings

It's the unknown that scares us.

We've been in the dark for so long,

we start perceiving it as our comfort zone.

It's not. It never was.

No matter how scary it may seem,

you need to take a step.

Just because you don't see your wings,

doesn't means, you don't have them.

They aren't always feathery moveable things attached at
your back.

Your wings, they are your blood.

your heart, that's beating, no matter what the situation is.

Your soul, that's always loyal.

That whisper, yelling at you to never give up.

You.

Stop searching your wings.

Stop searching for something, that's within you.

Start believing.

Treachery

we all go through some rotten luck, and it gets really impossible to endure. People show their true colors, people leave you, and judge you when you need them most.

The kind of treachery that rips your soul apart. It feels as if you're in such a deep dark pit, where there's no way out.

The one you love and feel for, leaves you with uncertainties, insecurities, and questions which have no answers.

You hold back, you hang in there, waiting, trying, but nothing happens.

Scars on the body can heal but oh, those scars bleeding the soul, what about them?

Survived

The scars on her soul were visible in her eyes.

you could feel it in her silence,
that the fire and the storm was real. . . and
You could feel in her gentle soft touch that she survived.